£4

THE CLEAVER GARDEN

GEORGE MACBETH

The Cleaver Garden

SECKER & WARBURG
LONDON

First published in England 1986 by
Martin Secker & Warburg Limited
54 Poland Street, London W1V 3DF

British Library Cataloguing in Publication Data

MacBeth, George
The cleaver garden.
I. Title
821'.914   PR6063.A13

ISBN 0–436–27014–5

Typeset by Inforum Ltd, Portsmouth
Printed in Great Britain by
Redwood Burn Ltd, Trowbridge

The Briton, fat with blood from school,
Being no sort of silly fool
Abhors the shapes of death and pain
Yet roams abroad to kill again.
There must be, to put matters plain,
A cleaver garden in his brain
Wherefrom, on all his country rambles,
He recreates the urban shambles.

– Robert Lloyd, from *The Chase*, 1762

CONTENTS

I

The Meat Market   xi

II

The Blooding Ring   25
The Scalpel House   51
The Skull Yard   75

III

The Slaughter Ground   99

FOREWORD

I have tried to deal with the fascinating sheen of blue steel, and the inflaming odour of blood and offal. Hence, the poem's opening with Smithfield, the cleaver garden's hot-house. I have ended with anywhere, the green belt for preference, where the popping of shot-guns is as frequent as the grapeshot of champagne corks. I don't imagine, of course, that England has been worse than other powers in its blood-thirstiness and cruelty, but one must put one's own house in order first. Roman discipline, which has ironed Europe, echoes in the girders of St Thomas's Hospital as menacingly as in the plastered marbles of Highgate Cemetery or along the pillared frontages of a hundred public schools. Hence, my middle section where the sanguinary prospects of these archetypal institutions are allowed their red mist. This is not exactly, however, a tract against meat-eating, or even blood-sports, metaphorical or otherwise. A savoury gravy splashes most rosy spectacles.

FOREWORD

THE MEAT MARKET

'You English trade in blood and guts as we Dutch deal in spices.'

– Admiral De Ruyter, after the Battle of Bergen, 1665.

I

You saw one corner from the train.
Its octagon got at you, grey as brain,
And now the juggernauts beside it block Long Lane

In emptying hugeness. Lights gleam wet
But no one seems to bother to work yet
Although a few men stand round laughing. They've just met,

It seems, to chin-wag about meat
And watch clouds hosing down the sky with sleet
That spoils their afternoon. On rubbered, muddy feet

They stroll between the pubs, or talk,
Or stand outside the cutlers' shops, or walk
In ordinary shoes, discussing sides of pork.

II

At night, speed changes. Then the dark
Seeps up from Holborn Viaduct, corpse-stark
Like something out of Mayhew's London, killer-shark.

A black shape rears. Its lolling tongue
Gashes red like a Rembrandt ox's lung
And, fouled with lights, smells high and badly hung.

This is the mood of Smithfield. Meat
Absorbs the form of what would find it sweet
And snuffles all its odour, and is out on heat.

The night resumes. After the still
Of day, blood gains a vigilance of will
And meat climbs back to gnaw its mutilated kill.

III

Be calm. Stay close to where the lights
  Allow an ease of passage, and eyes' whites
Convey the safety of slain carcases. The night's

  Offal is living. Out there, sick
  Things are on cobble slippery to lick.
They dip their wormy candles in each stuck pig's wick.

  Decades ago, they say. The moon's
  Shining now like an arc lamp on steel runes
Where scattered saw-dust mixed with spilled blood mounds
                                            in dunes.

  Now proper sanitation bans
  Those heaps of bowel that led rats to pans
And brought the rodent operatives round in vans.

IV

Even the War Memorial's nice
Lifting the butchery to sacrifice.
The names of those who died for Smithfield shine like spice.

Under a mediaeval shield
The glory of the cleaver stands revealed.
It "fought for England", on a gorgeous azure field.

It swung, a silver arc of fire
That burned those heroes in a bullshit mire
And seared off knees and shoulders by some Belgian spire.

Now it remains: a flame of red
Shed from the tongues of dragons overhead
Whose sculptured silver wings protrude like soldered lead.

V

God moved the hand of Horace Jones
Who built this temple out of blood and groans
Where dogs now grovel to their bellies, chewing bones.

It soars, clean Greek. Its Portland white
And steak-red brick and iron blued chime right
Against a black sheep sky, a shepherd's raw delight.

The tripled colours of the Flag
Repeat here in the crimson on a rag
A cleaver's wiped on, blue, imperial. But this brag

Of butchery, like a blood-slaked map
Or stretch of spinning globe winched from a trap
And laid in fee for livestock, lashes like a strap.

VI

It stains its environs. A field
Of force, or energy, fleshes its yield.
A cold store sports encaustic tiles, a cartouche shield.

Below, chipped iron doors. A wall
Stripped of its windows lingers like a caul.
Outside, an organ-grinder's monkey minds the stall.

But that was yesterday. Today
The same grey, raw-faced draymen pout and sway
Behind their cloudy beer. The same lean tom-cat sprays.

But something's different. Machines
As faceless as that wall no bent hose cleans
Enclose their frozen beef. Deaf drivers chew baked beans.

VII

Meat costs more now. The empty rich
Cull each iced baron. Sweating from the ditch
Where good rump ran with blood, the aproned leaders itch.

A girl goes by. Under the heat
Of burning neon, everyone thinks, meat.
This is the meat market. They watch her twinkling feet

Like stars along the offal. Eyes
Go back to notebooks, or to peas and fries.
The prostitutes head out of Smithfield, if they're wise.

Meat breeds a rage. Unsheathed, knives glare
And jokes like whips are cracked in foetid air
Where horns are ground to powder, heels to glue. Men stare.

VIII

Night gathers to its peak. The coins
And notes are counted, and the friable loins
Are settled in their baking-joists. No cat purloins.

A carter wipes his brow. A side
Of mutton gives a droning fly a ride.
The tanner-master flogs his wares, a pound a hide.

Or did. His present skins are cured
And packed in crates, and suitably insured,
And sent – they say dispatched – far from where hearts are
skewered.

Hygiene is rife. The days of guts
Are over, like the days of hubs and ruts
When waggonloads of waste were rummaged for nice cuts.

IX

Now cleanness rules. Proud of their looks
Labourers lift hogs, headless, onto hooks
Of burnished steel. No tinge of blood sours pigs for cooks

Or leaves them less than prime. The glance
Of idle buyers glides on clots askance
And movements of the mind require no sanguinary trance.

Not any more. None see the slabs
Of grey-veined marble when the Dane's jaw grabs
Its deemed right meat. These halls are clinical as labs.

Men move in white coats now. Blue stripes
On aprons are as obsolete as tripes
And innards are disposed of through soft, plastic pipes.

X

Noise means a shearing. Someone hones
A separating-blade on whetted stones.
Someone else with a slicer in his waist-belt phones.

The iron hand in the hanging clock
Over the central aisle shudders. The shock
Of hearing ten struck makes the talkers pause, take stock.

Sounds, monitory in pungent air
Sick with an undertang as in a lair,
Echo, then, smothered in rank flesh, turn vague and tear.

Sounds form a prelude. Sound of blades
Or talk of blades, or flickering of grades
Of Sheffield steel, or German grinding. Knives do trades.

XI

Across the road, supporting shops
Glisten with tempting. But no worker stops.
Not now. The clockhand's blunted cleaver mounts and chops.

Behind plate glass where blades are splayed
Like sunbursts on a wheel, my gaze feels flayed.
I stare until the glass dissolves, and sun breeds shade,

And Smithfield Sheffield. And I seem
To see again our blunt Ford in a dream
And slip, selling, and quote United as my team.

Dour days, those were. On blood like ice
I offered sharpness to men slaughtering. Mice
Were all I'd seen killed up till then. Pigs was less nice.

XII

Here nothing's killed: only frail time
Slain on the clockface by each quarter chime
And aerosoled flies. Meat comes regular as rhyme

Out of the ice-crates in the trucks
With neither ear nor hoof, nor any muck's
Imprint along its flanks. Cleaned meat. What sucks

And what was walked on sliced away
And sold as dog-food, and the rest, a ray
Of bland and yellowy coldness, hung to pray.

You might say crucified. But no.
That Roman punishment, though dire and slow,
Required nail-worthy limbs. These lost theirs hours ago.

XIII

The killing happens elsewhere. Swords
Arch in a battle-sky where straining cords
Hug horses to their guns. Gluttony stamps the board.

The redcoats falter, and the line
Thin as a cut lies sacrificed for chine
Where soldiers, mesmerised by sabres, die like swine.

Poultry we call hens: beef those cows
Not used for milk. When someone stoops, he bows:
And mutton with its throat slit slimes the slaughterhouse.

Nothing is what it is. By names
We purify the aroma of what shames.
Pork squeals in French. This is the abattoir that maims.

XIV

Here we divide the spoils; by joints
Whose weight and shape no memory anoints
Rinse resonance of meadows. Gristle gains no points

Nor does the glistening of an eye.
Shoulder is something tasty that you fry.
Chicken-meat sells to chicks who shop from Peckham Rye.

Comedy rules. Poor puns are rife:
The one about the horsemeat butcher's wife;
Whore's-meat. Then, Jews and pork. Straw-hatted to the life,

Each red-armed salesman draws his breath
Unbothered by his industry of death
Or in-bred jokes: prime lamb of God – from Nazareth.

XV

It covers the whole block. Walk round,
You walk round England. In a sea of ground
Its traffic never stops. Tyres make a hissing sound,

Skin slips, gates clang. Opening doors
Exude faint stench from impregnated floors.
On stone, above the pediment, Britannia snores.

One incident shows all. A rack of ribs
Brings scribbling of a hundred busy nibs
To a standstill. One backer, baulked by false scales, jibs.

Tempers flare. And a bunched fist shoves.
Raw-faced and roaring, "arseholes" swapped for "loves",
The backer hams it up, chest pouting like a dove's.

Pigeons fly over: and look down
On this; heartache of a mediaeval town
Where a foul soup still seethes. Britannia's lions crown

Each corner point, a watchful pride.
The concentration floor spreads out inside.
There lie the avenues, flame-crossed: each twelve feet wide

And smoothed for trolleys. Huge, wheeled slings
Trundle on rubber-soled, dead-silent rings
To shift the imperial produce. Each hanged bullock swings

In a cradle, purged of sperm and piss.
He dangles in clean air. Soft as a kiss
A handback brushes him: our bag of meat from Diss.

XVII

There on a drain-bank in the sun
They enjoyed a two-week summer. Though burned dun,
They chewed used blades of barley. Hearing someone's gun

    Sniping for pheasant, they flicked ears.
    Death didn't matter, they had years and years.
But summer passed, and night came. They were frightened
                                steers,

    Yarded, then driven up a ramp
    Into a slatted lorry. They could stamp
And voice their freedom, bellowing to the wintry camp,

    Steaming, and close together: all
    As ignorant as giants from Nepal
Packed off to the Antarctic to be frozen small.

XVIII

The overseer at his stall
Shakes out his water, and admires the wall.
Tiled, piped with copper, it sweats drops. Now blue jets fall

To cleanse the channel. Brass and chrome
Adorn this grand, Horatian androdrome
Where upright figures empty Guinness. Urines foam

To stain the china. Hauled-on zips
Contain the surge of bursting pizzles. Nips
Adjust what otherwise might flout girls' close-pursed lips

And offer meat injections. Meat!
One man is beating his. The wooden seat
Rocks to his rhythm. I can hear him neigh and bleat.

XIX

Later, on tables, carved and fine,
We chicken folk are eaten with cold wine.
Slobbering faces drag us from the crouching line

And gnash their teeth. No lease of scope
Allows their honesty to seem a grope
For any joy. It soils us, like a hangman's rope.

They want our faeces. What we own
Is bartered like a 'twenties gramophone
Whose only record, stolen from life, is of a groan.

In under fifteen minutes, gone
Like offal or manure, our skeleton
And all it held is eaten. Appetite slides on.

XX

Look. A raw streak there in the east,
The slit of Dawn: the prostitute of yeast
Whose rising hams provide. Smithfield suborns no priest

In yoking with her. Mistress Dawn
Whose fingers "pull the curtain all forlorn"
Is not for here. Poetry comes less free than porn.

The draymen, wakeful, sniff the air.
They want their breakfast, and they smell it there
Under the cold smell of the butcher's, hot and bare.

They take it hard and fast: then eat
Like lustful boys who do it with their feet
And save their bacon, prudent; and then stroll the street.

XXI

The Norsemen with their cups of horn
And women with portmanteaux not yet born
And farmers in their boots, who deal in beet and corn

All use ancillaries. Those parts
We cannot eat are woven. Girls at Bart's
Across the road sport uniforms. Off-duty, hearts

Burst for their bums in leather. Bulls
Abused in dying bring them hide that pulls,
Tauric. They like it better than their earnest wools.

Those leave the sheep unharmed. They let
It range again. Blood needs what it can get:
Something more lethal to pay off its tingling debt.

XXII

Air seeps with the infection. Wind
Savours the tragedy of being skinned
And wafts a spore to other places. Wasted, thinned

In what it offers, blood runs cold
At Billingsgate, where fish are bought and sold
And all its coronary wares grow weak and old

In Covent Garden, land of beans,
Where laden baskets mask a world of greens
And brave King Edwards gather, shredded by machines.

Eyes blink in fancifulness. Talk
Summons the vegetarians, sharp as chalk.
Stay, though. Recall the jungle on a single stalk.

XXIII

All dies. Only the seed of meat
 Sown in the loins of women, fouled on heat,
Erects its monument of rust. Blades crisp as wheat

 Slither in dipping to their slice
 And leave a taste as bitter as bad rice
While stiff annihilation hinges down its vice.

 Death is a glory to the blood
 That rains in hope of empire turned to mud.
But still the living ruminant will chew his cud.

 Smithfield's the guts he meanders through.
 Death's like a passage: yes, an avenue
Towards a noble house, that fronts a lovely view.

No, it's not that easy. Torn scars
Trouble the old elms, and the aching stars,
And even mortar. Dry rot mounts the enclosing spars

That anchor Smithfield. Iron rots
And stone disintegrates, and history blots
Out both the captive-bolt gun and the carving-slots

Where men stand cattle. But the kill
Finds other outlets. Buckets fill with swill
Of vomit, and the messes of the mortal spill.

It keeps going. We have to watch
And drown our sorrows at it in good Scotch:
And try to slow it down: and make some details botch.

THE BLOODING RING

"I've known nothing to equal this since I was at Winchester."

> – English officer, writing home to his
> mother, after the Battle of the Somme, 1916

I

It rules your life now. It becomes
The Colosseum where your stomach strums
To the rim of pain. Here is the arena of bared gums.

Here the raw legionaries play
At what will later on fill out their day.
They slaughter lambs. They practise their young ass's bray.

Here the old consuls tap their fists
Flexing a bull's-hide thong on puckered wrists.
Cold sweat glistens. They scratch their festering crust,
                                        their cysts.

Here is the amphitheatre
Where deaf Rome drops her thumbs. Fame can inter
Only the deadest Christians. But live lions purr.

II

Remember, then, the flying pitch
Where dirt shone blacker than a bacon-flitch
And being blooded stained your shirt. Which brush was which,

Yours or the fox's? Buying meat,
The butchers learn to cross their laces neat
And blood comes down from Sandhurst like a flood of sleet.

Remember this. It's flagstaff time
And grubbier boys attentive to the slime
Are trying to make up a cruder, lewder rhyme

To tart the school song. Thews that lie
And cumber never thrive. For thew, write thigh.
Fondle the Flag like football knickers. Tease the sky.

III

This is Remembrance Day. Blind meat
In all its stuffed pomposity, élite
Like any Christmas turkey, trots on tawny feet

And sweats a tear. This is the day
When older boys resume their games for pay
And younger, evil ones their interrupted play,

In clustered ranks, the platform kind
Swoop down like mustard on that bin of rind,
The orange-juice-fed faces of the lightly dined.

Friends. I repeat, friends, noble men.
You gorged the worst the school could serve us then
And (huge applause) survived it with the guts of ten.

IV

Remember. Lay your flag of blood
As crimson as a cow's tongue slick on mud.
Rhyme it with anything. With rose-bud, or with crud.

It means the same. It means the Flag,
The stone of waving England, Heaven's hag,
Whose wilting soldiers know two true tricks, how to shag

And how to die. Oh, it still comes
To the same end, thin mustering by drums
And a long dereliction of the Scottish slums.

Glasgow, avaunt. Ride south and win.
Your public school shines brighter than a pin.
Listen. That squeal's your destiny, its luring din.

V

The school-bell rings. Whatever you are,
Desperate or hopeful, catamite or star,
You are mirrored in her forcing-field, its nenuphar.

You, lily-livered, stalk her plot.
You, lily-featured, see her as a blot
Against a sky of slate, a sunburst like a clot.

Mother of learning, and of grief,
Red-handed as a dying maple leaf,
She's randy with her empire, blood-sick past belief.

It's butcher's, wheel it. Stone the crows
And sell the ring-doves into slavery. Those
Who come to toughen up must learn to touch their toes.

VI

Look to your merlons on the Hill,
Your cars that dip in passing to the kill,
Your systematic lodging-houses, knots of will.

Feint from the caper, and the cane,
The pith of reason that will clog your brain.
Be bloody, brave and resolute. Honour means gain.

Thus drones your old school, where you were.
Where you were what? Were slavering like a cur
Or flogged with bright spurs? Here you learned to call men, sir.

Here you were new. Here, later, knew
Slang for the Woodbine's creep, the joke struck blue
To ignite the stinking backs, the bud of Housman's rue.

VII

Nothing much happened, though. Not much.
 Only the rabbit's scramble for its hutch
When the sharp weasels came, their claws out for the crotch.

 Balls fouled with dubbin, blubbing, stop
 One felt a hard belt like a razor-strop.
Another fought back, fool. Boys weighed him for the drop.

 One night they got him, four by two,
 And slung him in a cellar. Four could spew,
Two hung his body, and whipped him. Brawl home, sniffing
                                                          glue,

 You later louts, your eyes like stoats',
 You slate friends in your Crombie overcoats,
Pig-headed as young pigs, plug-ugly as old goats.

VIII

Bullying starts things. It can rent
A premise in the ringworm. What was meant
As a light-headed romp ends up a tournament.

The whistle blows. All sanctions fail
And Eton is as bad as Passchendaele.
The pederastic shell-bursts blossom. Frankly male

You may be, but forced running yields
Female physiques. Boys start from Furness Fields.
Cross-country through the mud they flounder for steel shields.

Life is a battle. School is war
And heroes are begotten by that roar.
Listen. The dying lions yell for more and more.

IX

Arse-wiper Barton has the floor.
Saw-dusted for a dance it holds the Corps.
Air-training turns boys blue. They shiver, or they snore,

Hearing him rant. That sneering beak
Fresh here from Repton's trying to look chic
Head-hunters claim to think. But then, no head's a freak.

In a school, he began, quite soft,
Of this calibre, his right hand raised aloft –
And most of us rose cheering. But one young Jew coughed.

He was the boy who never came
To School Assembly. Cohen was his name:
Outcast from paradise by the eternal flame.

X

That holocaust caught up the cool.
It warmed their cheeks, abused the swimming-pool.
Spoiled in his trunks, one ducked love's elementary rule:

Don't sneak. So dried his unseen tears
And learned the use of hands, and pricking ears,
And, when the pilling epidemic broke out, shopped his peers.

Expelled, in the army some won gongs.
Others, in dreams, raped girls in green sarongs,
Remembering. That treachery still floats in songs,

But the school endures. New virgins rise
With fresh erections and even dirtier ties.
The dormitories fester. Fags are scored like tries.

XI

Arms slope. Eyes right. The columned line
Promotes an excellence, looks rather fine.
Fagging's an honour system. It behoves you swine

To do your homework. Masters swot
The next page in their joke-book. If you spot
Their errors, then you get it. Better to pick your snot

And nod. The interested win.
The losers are the ones who scratch a shin
And lift their voices. Please, sir, Pompey didn't win.

Nor you. You rise, put out your hand,
And take a pasting you can scarcely stand.
It raises weals along your life-line. Beatings brand.

XII

Go back, then. Walk down Clarkehouse Road
And stalk them for their colours, gay with woad,
Your heirs, your game. Their Walkmans bluster notes in code,

They coil entranced. Centurion hair
Catches prescriptive glances, dims your glare
To a staccato crimson. Ghetto-blasters blare.

Walk on. Don't mess with trends, dear boy.
They only make their noises to annoy.
Grant them their cobolt dyes and dreadlocks. Wish them joy.

Thus *l'ancien régime*. Blue rinse
Is what it proffers, like a plate of mince.
But stuffed with rare blue sirloin, lionesses wince.

XIII

Girls change, though. Well, were our girls girls?
They came with such eccentric, whipped-cream curls
And some of them wore twin-sets, or had cultured pearls.

Those were girls' times. Boys danced in halls
Under a spill of diamonds, huge balls
That scattered will-o-the-wisps. Girls brushed you with their
shawls,

If they were hot. If not, you wanked
Your way home in a taxi, fully tanked.
You were dizzy with disgust, and gin. If you were thanked,

If was for being a sport. No date
Ever put her own florin in the plate.
You were the boss. You paid. The cavalry came too late.

XIV

Now the boot's on the other foot. I watch
Boys jostle by, glazed skin like butterscotch.
Voici venir l'année de l'androgyne. They blotch

Eyes with a kind of kohl. I itch
To speculate. Which one of them is which?
This dame in lipstick, or this drag queen he called Mitch

With a parasol? Garters merge,
Become suspenders, grate your calves like serge.
The amphisbaenae nudge near, and the trams converge.

Collisions build. In fruitful silk
I see Boy George vindictive at his milk
While Sting invents a cobra suckling Charlie Dilke.

XV

Woe. Snakes of such reined fancy pall.
There isn't any eagerness to install.
History's *passé*. Kids like Wham, not Aspinall.

    So go alone. Get back inside
Up your stamped flight of steps inflating pride.
Suffer the urns to offer you a ride. Then slide

    In the Hall. School Office, mate. Still there
Prinked in its alcove opposite the stair.
Stale where it always was. Pens couple. Ink-wells pair.

    But, no they don't. It's biros now
The office offers, calculators plough
The furrowed brow. The seeds of knowledge waft from Slough.

XVI

Go across the tiles, echoing, slow,
Let your feet allow you to be long ago.
Through the glass doors, glide up. The cups are glistening,
　　　　　　　　　　　　　　　　　　　　　though,

They're high. The gallery swirls round
Several feet above the familiar ground
Where desks have replaced benches, gossiping boys the pound

Of the school's organ. Fleece is shorn.
The little lambs eat ivy, gorge on corn.
You make sheep's eyes for nothing. The mink hair shirt's torn,

Your agony's all adrift. So turn
Into your hail of memory. Tears churn
For what was never worth it. Will they never learn?

XVII

They spit their way from drains too deep.
They gather energy from those who sleep.
They ponce for dreams. They bring you crops you loathe
                                        to reap.

They satisfy a kind of truth
Wrung from that Roman sponge, the book of ruth.
Tears ache for nothing like the nerve inside a tooth.

Tears glow. They wipe the filthy past.
They blow nostalgia to a horny blast.
They cast a cold eye like a cold eye with a cast.

I let them come, I suck my fill.
I pluck a cupful from their overspill
And feel a nervous, elemental, sober thrill.

XVIII

Sour tears: then tears of passion come
Sawing the air on skids, learning to slum;
Tears that are far too high, too fine, to splash a drum;

Tears to exalt you, drawing dole
From the plumbed heroes who were never whole,
Those on the primrose path, who burned their blood for coal

Like Carding-Wells. A motor-bike
Decapitated him across a dyke
On the road to Eaton Hall. Death filed him on a spike.

Others, too. Other boys I knew
Spring tears. One who could chalk a billiard cue.
One boy at least with long-lashed eyes. He tops the queue.

XIX

Enough. You can't go on to weep,
The very word sounds phoney, makes flesh creep.
You have to crawl back raving. School was just a heap.

Suppose you won. Became Head Boy
In your last year, with all that power to annoy:
Beat the old beating record. You'd say, rule's a joy,

You bastard. So the beaten think,
Watching your muzzles as you stoop to drink,
You power-laden few. But rebellion makes a stink,

They knuckle under. And the School
Slides on, magnificently rich, and cool.
But sick. Sick as a Lord, who needs his dog to rule.

XX

I had my dogs. Twelve made a gang
Enough to fill a football charabanc.
King Edward's mercenaries, we prevailed by slang.

Week after week, we worked the grounds,
Wednesday's or United's, blazered hounds.
Adsett's choc-ices broke the crackling. Gropes cost pounds.

Rivalry jack-knifed into pride,
Kneading our dates, fawning on dough. We'd tried,
Trying was all. You took your virginity for a ride,

Fiddled the change. Shagged, if you could:
And, if the date seemed ugly, used a hood
And gave no name; and, if the dough gleamed plenty, stood.

XXI

Some stood a lot. Emerged as boss
 Of a small empire gaudy with the gloss
Of what elsewhere meant honour, like a minor schloss

Mimicking Hampton Court. The clique
 Who ruled the school wore waistcoats. Some, unique
In yellow, smouldered. Lickspittle fear played hide-and-peek

As they strolled the corridors. Shoes ruled
 Wielded as welting slippers. Passions cooled
And fancies totted up. Resources were well spooled.

Thus it was always. Thus it may
 Be still. The Roman prefects, and the sway
Of lashes make our brutal institutions pay.

XXII

How does the illness come, though? How
Can meat by rugby-playing thus endow
Its chain-mail with new choir-boys, needling then to now?

The stitches weaken, yes. But soon
The stitchers fight back, by a grinning moon,
And each worm-eaten Stilton stinks by to a tune.

The ripeness gathers. And the smell
Enters the flaring eardrums like a knell.
Boys bite, and learn. Then enter blithely, as to hell.

The stiff machine-guns mow. But still
Boys walk ahead, blood-boltered, to the mill
Where the toothed grindstones grind them, like a dentist's drill.

XXIII

Leaving, the last Assembly's death.
You use it like your mother's dying breath
Or the last battle in your namesake play, *Macbeth*.

Too serious for what it seems,
It is. A licence to a last act of screams
Preceded by the nightmare horseplay of your dreams:

Dreams, and a pageantry where all
Six hundred stand and gallop as you fall
And the cups overhead ring down Night's final pall:

Dreams, and the entrance to more rooms
Where Life has set you further tasks and dooms
And an immense, oracular, black Absence looms.

THE SCALPEL HOUSE

"Almost on the threshold of the twentieth century, the chief instruments of English surgery were the leech and the cauterising blade."

– Sir John Chinnery, *A Doctor's Apology*, 1939

I

It squats beside the river. Cross
The bridge and you can feel the gust of loss
Flung out above the sloping mud-flats like coal dross.

On crenels of their gain, the few
Who enter and come out stand strong and new.
Fortified by their pain, they plant will like a shoe.

Some you can meet, advancing. Some
Lean on the rail, and practise to succumb.
A few just watch Westminster, or the water, numb.

These are the lucky ones. The dead
Are drawn away by night. No prayers are said.
Like anthracite, they go in bags, with no tears shed.

II

Losing is bad manners. The ones
Who shout, I'm dying, to their wives and sons
And close their eyes, gain no reward. Their panic stuns.

The wards shiver. A well-versed nurse
Glides up on silent heel-stubs like a hearse.
Everything has to rhyme with guts. What could be worse

Than someone screaming, Help, than hands
That reach for buzzers, lights that glow like glands?
They grant injections. They connive with choking strands

Grasping for entrails. Pain perturbs
The concentration, like parked cars by kerbs.
A world war starts, and they're not caring. We're just Serbs.

III

You go from Waterloo past miles
Or so it seems, of tiny, earth-grey tiles;
Count the appalled graffiti, lewd. Maggie's like piles,

Bugger the lot. The same perverse
Expostulations mar both sides. It's worse
If you're a woman. But, the whole world's got the curse.

At the entrance, waiting for a bone,
A lion in reconstituted stone
Looks south. Boudicca's chariot pairs it, a black throne.

Launched in a wind, haunched down. Oh, black
And dispiriting as that ramp your slow soles hack.
This is your Calvary to crucifix and rack.

IV

Strike for the chapel. The great board
Of former surgeons glitters, a coin hoard
Of sovereigns. But those gilt-less names have been restored.

Below in the hall their igniting busts
Glower white on basalt columns, burned like crusts.
They severed at the breast. They moulder in their dusts.

Now bland successors dawdle by,
Each with a knighthood in his gimlet eye
And something more: the means to make a century die.

Well to the right Victoria sits
As comfortably stoned as if she knits,
Wise woman. In the drill of Fame, crowns rust like bits.

V

Four years ago I came here first
Chasing a sort of coronary thirst.
Someone I knew was losing platelets. Nothing burst

Or broke and bled. But not for long.
The echo of that illness grew too strong.
It struck her inner breastwork. She could hear the gong

And came to die. The corrupt cells
Tackled her in a place of jinxing spells
Where only needles mattered. She could watch the bells

Chime at St Margaret's, comb her gold
Hair. But the river claimed her. She was sold.
Nothing could bring her back. She was too bored and cold.

VI

Not fair. No. But the fear of this
Makes nursing seem a mere parenthesis
Where life and hope slide by. We cure death with a kiss

And wax the body. Onto a slab
Those who control the acids and the lab
Tip out the ordered human residues. They dab

On powder, douse stench. And this new
Creation of our skill joins the slow queue
Waiting to go down to the chapel. Filing through

With daffodils, we relatives
Look at our shining prize as if it lives.
We pass by, tearful. And a creaking floorboard gives.

VII

Outside, spread shoulders. Plump, alive,
The bereaved watch the seagulls glide and dive.
Seagulls have a hard time. They have to pinch and strive.

We watch them, thinking. Over there
Our masters in their lighted chambers care.
They do, don't they? I mean, they try to make things fair.

The equal arches gleam. Big Ben
Looms like a massive clitoris. Those men
And women whom we voted in besmirch their pen.

Like sheep, they cringe at whips. Like goats
Who know nothing, pursue their bags of oats.
So we bereaved muse, soured in our dark, wintry coats.

VIII

Behind our back, the krankenhaus
Block by long block commands the shore. No louse
Allowed in there would last. No sewage-rat, nor mouse.

Order presumes. At proper hours
The plumbers come to investigate the showers.
The canteen-cleaners match their trays. In spiralling towers

Even the ordure knows its place,
Vanishes into nowhere, leaves no trace.
The aluminium is polished, shows your face.

The doctor comes. As though on wheels
Like a trolley, he revolves, says what he feels
And slides on. Health has shown us a clean pair of heels.

IX

Once I was in their grip. The war
Had taught me rheumatism like semaphore.
Pulse was a wavering tendril. Legs were stiff and sore.

MacIntyre thought. Then frowned and said,
You're better off the way you are in bed.
He was wrong, though. I might have been, more truly, dead.

The Royal took me. Iron-green,
With someone deaf inside a lung-machine.
The ward rode with the dying. Life was too obscene

For those. They laughed. One told a joke
About the sister that he'd like to poke.
One in his mind bestrode me. But I never spoke.

X

That was the last year of the war.
I escaped with a bad heart. Luck like ore
Accrued under my arteries. I've come no more.

Others have been. Some came for birth
In a profound, slow leavening of earth
And some for operations to control their girth.

Worlds have tumbled. Globes have spun
And Thomas's deliveries have begun
In an awning of blue uniforms. Birth can be fun.

Birth is a blazon of blood's choice
Under a glaze of ribbon, like a voice
Crying, dear father, unto you a son. Rejoice.

XI

A cleaver cut mine open. Brought
Nearer to torture than she'd yet been taught
His mother twisted while the electric shocks grew short.

The machines rallied. She cried out,
I want to go home now. But nurses flout
Your sufferings. You have to dim each frightened shout

And learn to wait. They guess at last
The hour of her accouchement has gone past.
Nothing to do but cut. And so the die is cast

And the child born. Thus Caesar came
Torn from his mother's womb by labouring flame.
Cauterised and hygienic, scalpels delve the same.

XII

I was there. If you'd seen her, you'd
Understand why all hospitals feel crude.
They look to me like anguish-slates. They bear the snood

Of a religious chance, a will
To slaughter, and the order of a kill
And blood rolls through their corridors like chlorophyll.

Sometimes to cure, I know. Sometimes
It dims the batteries to a snail of chimes
And cracks the clockwork of a liver. Hopes grow crimes

When someone like your mother spoils
In a ridiculous blunderland of oils.
A jungle grows inside. A chalk-nosed python coils.

XIII

Now I've come back. After all those
Blank years of absence filtered by the rose
I return for a simple operation on my nose.

An Indian, when I enquired
What was up there, said, polyps. It transpired
I had one polyp. The news left me hinged and wired.

Operate, yes. But not too soon.
Let indolence vacate me, a bassoon.
Play a few notes of blockage first. Bore out a tune.

So winter trembles by. No smells
Wither the silence when the nostril swells.
A dead odour pervades, ghost ozone breathed from shells.

XIV

It's time. Enter the sanctum, clean.
Washed in hot water, I feel coped and lean.
Nose cleared with Vick inhaler, mouth with listerine,

I parade. Enough clothes for two nights
And pyjamas, which I never sport, by rights
Unnecessary, stack my suitcase. Girls wear tights

I notice now, not stockings. Two
Giggle around the corner, in full view.
I drop my trousers while their jokes are burning blue.

Then lights out. And I lie awake,
Hands below head, and angry, for God's sake.
What will they do to me? How badly will I ache?

XV

Back here, tomorrow, I shall learn
After the first injection, then the stern
Injunction to relax. Oh yes, I shall return

Rolled up asleep on metal, then
Put back in bed, the cynosure of men,
Watched by the rueful soldiers who must go again.

Waking, to feel the blush of air
Startle the chambers that were cobwebbed, bare,
And stank of mould, I shall feel grateful. That I swear.

But fearful too. Yes, I forgot
Three hours, and lay like prawns put in a pot,
Oblivious of reason, raving, polyglot.

XVI

I ask. They only smile, though, kind.
They see so many who have lost their mind.
It doesn't matter. Delirium is undefined.

This is the crazy house. You lose
Your money here in betting on the clues.
Each operation is a sort of mystery cruise.

Captain, avaunt. I pace the decks
Under a mist of dissipated sex.
The small ones with the moles beneath their knickers vex.

Forget it. You'll go home today.
Loom at the window. Feel your sea-waist sway.
Practise your elegance, your sniffing. Odours pray.

XVII

Now on the bridge I stand. Look back
At what seem quarters of a building-pack:
Some bombed; some reconstructed; some just space, and lack

Of money to make grass be stone.
I draw the salt in, blow the telephone
Of an aroma courteous as friendly bone.

This is sheer life. I see the House
Of Lords there like a moor swept clear of grouse;
The garden of the Thames grown green. Oh, to have nous

And own the power of what these do.
It isn't all a vicious parvenu
Exacting vengeance. Or a canzonet in glue.

XVIII

They do the best they can. They scour
The worst, and leave the well-pruned part to flower.
It isn't always possible to stem its power.

It grows. It reaches for all things
With a swart myriad of warps and stings.
It agonises as a duty. Torps and wrings

Tendrils too dense with vomit, foul
As any wound-pus that would make you howl.
It scatters what it gathers, and it shrouds the cowl

It bears. It comes, though, and it quakes.
It spews its venom like a bed of snakes.
What it will have is blood. It rakes us, and it breaks.

XIX

Shudder. Then use your poetry skill.
Drip words like acid on a window-sill.
Defeat your sibilance like serpents, if you will.

Farming the geese out of his boat
One lord from Lincolnshire learned how to gloat.
Ducked esses squawked like adders, and then dammed his moat.

Thus came the castle style. No clue
To where those cows of Cooper's learned to moo
Comes out of Cowper, though. Crabbe's names, too, bloat *Who's
Who.*

Poetry tinkers. Tinkers curse
And both the people and their thing clink worse
Than plated silver. Milkless pain inspires no nurse.

XX

When does a doctor cry for Vaughan?
The Tennyson most need is on their lawn.
Coal blacks knights' rackets. Bishops vacillate in pawn.

It gives the lie to every wit
Whose plot fails in the puncturing of the pit.
The public yawns. Where medicine judgemental sits

All versifiers drain their glass
And pass, blood-donors, from the fencing-class.
Let others probe and settle. We can cut the grass

Or smoke it. In a haze of dope
The dazzling orreries of magic slope
And planets yet unknown appear, and jilted sisters mope.

XXI

Nothing cures nothing. Verse bled white
Observes no reticence before what's trite.
No decent intervals convene. The soft cells fight.

Write then. More accurately than
The copywriter if you really can:
Tight as a tourniquet, clear as a fever-scan.

Let surgery supply. The grave
Where Vaughan lies buried is an autoclave.
Blood swirls to help there. But the heart's valves crest their
wave.

Save where you can. Remember Keats,
Whose cadences drawl sweet as sugar-beets.
He loved the knife. His passion is a drug that treats.

XXII

Too eighteenth century, you'll say:
Too many moods personified away
Like marble statues hijacked, and then fudged from clay:

Too many clever, obvious rhymes
Adjusted to lobbed rhythms like fixed chimes
Of an old clock that only tells of former times,

Won't go. Why bother, when there's prose
And aspirin? It's all artifice, it shows,
And here and there, I'd say, you've stolen people's clothes.

Witch-doctor's robes, perhaps. But then
All crib from skulls and bones who push a pen.
Readers crave bodies. We're the resurrection-men.

THE SKULL YARD

"If the location of the plague pits is examined, the whole of London can be seen as one vast cemetery."

– R.K. Widdiscombe, *The Middle Ages*, 1954

I

A number beckon. One I choose
Burns down from Highgate on a dwindling fuse.
Ears prick. The cat of memory too softly mews.

Neglect refuses to give place.
Tombs lean. Drenched ivy lends a certain grace
To what might otherwise seem scaled, and losing face.

But vandalism flowers, too.
The trowel of renovation squirrels through
To what was once a cannery, a place to screw.

We lovers yield. Our failing screams
Orgasmic to the night tear at the seams
And, somewhere in the soil, an answering passion steams.

II

Today no beckoning of a child
Reintroduces what was once too wild.
Memorials on the hill darken, unreconciled.

A statue kneeling with a spike
Stark in the air creates a trope too like.
This headless boy who died too young to ride a bike

Reminds me. And the freshened flowers
Wet where a freshened grieving for him scours
Appal. More transitory than most human powers

Love settles to its pile of stones,
Its abstract geometry of holes and cones,
The final wifely energy that sometimes phones.

III

Knowing this, and the roads to it,
I pick a Sunday, and I do my bit,
Revisiting the scenes glimpsed from the arrow-slit,

The keep of Highgate Hill. Dead rain
Battles with anguish on a window-pane.
The footsoles grapple, while the eyelids grope and strain.

Marvell lived here. Ben Jonson died
Near where we made our start. Oh my young bride
I take you now for always. How could cold clay slide?

I see the failing urns, the earth
In torment, and the mirror of your mirth.
Never betray those times, nor parody their worth.

IV

It's steep to climb. Drowned years ago
I bussed up from the Underground below
At Archway. And the gradient made anger glow.

The Nag's Head's closed now. Afternoon
Grates on the tinkle of a blistered spoon.
My lungs are heaving like an old barrage balloon.

I pay and leave. Waterlow Park
Fronts a low dish-shape in the gathering dark
And Marx's brows behind the railings beckon, stark.

Others lie here. But the great mind
Of German insolence that grew refined
And launched a world on sugar halts and draws the blind.

V

Spears raise their points. Around fouled graves
Where dogs have lost their courage, a wind raves.
Cold memory howls down a rotunda's architraves.

The heart owns a foreboding. Pain
At being here grows vaguer than a stain.
A hopeless longing floods like mud from a blocked drain.

Somewhere a gate clangs. A thrush comes
Along the avenue in search of crumbs.
An awkward stickiness afflicts my drying gums.

This is the toothache of the visitor
Who feels no penitential wound still sore
But visits anyway, vampire-like, needing gore.

VI

It's the same with all graveyards. Who
  Could say he went when scoring grief burned through?
Time turns the dying gas of pain to lower blue.

  Then stones provide. An arm of flowers
  Reached to the gravel satisfies frail powers
And a sense of having done the right thing flaunts its towers.

  The mourner walks away. The sun goes down
  And means of feeling better flush the town.
Tears' beetles dropped in boiling coffee twitch and drown.

  Guilt prickles. But the grieving heart
  Allows itself a sort of standing start.
You've bowed your head, and wept. You've stood, and played
                                        your part.

VII

I touch granite. It shines grey
Like what my mother called brawn yesterday:
The unfraying thread that keeps the dead stones yards away.

Bone yards, rather. Here anyone
Who needs the solace of a Christian pun
Can feel his finger grate on silence that will stun.

An urn rises. Its fluted sides
Hint at the wastes the crematorium hides.
Below its base a plinth of cheaper concrete slides.

Above its rim, a few stale blooms
Decorate air as if the air had rooms.
A bonfire of their shrivelled sisters creaks and fumes.

VIII

No one I know lies here. I lack
The pressure of real memory at my back
As I tour down the graves. Soot's turned some almost black

As if the love's perpetual flame
That some of these pumped owners like to name
Had lit and blackened artifice when it first came.

I feel shame, though: to see neglect
Of noble blood-lines, and grand history wrecked.
Gravel lies unraked. Ironwork is cracked, rust-flecked.

But so is mine. Far off, I know,
In Crookes, where my two close ones rest below
Their tumbled rims, the clock of care has run too slow.

IX

It often does. Curved ivy spires
And crinkles round the draperies of our sires.
It masks blotched rubbings on reliefs of breasts and choirs.

As here. The groin of beauty leans
On clutching balls of black seeds, fists of greens
Hoarding an ancient remonstrance, a swatch that cleans.

Flesh seethes in stone. A woman's arms
Ache in endeavours that betray soured charms
Above a spouse whose Adam's bulge no oak leaf calms.

The tombs remember. Stained with frost
And steeped in lime-leaf poison, bronze-embossed
Or pigeon-dropping-tinted, they loom sadly lost.

X

Victoriana shatters. Rose
And lily in the tiled work twine like hose.
The William Morris magic weaves a ghost, then snows.

A heart throbs. Passions breathe a cloud.
A songbird seems to pipe a dirge out loud.
The angel of the Lord waves off a sullen crowd

In ivory. Policeman-like,
Our Saviour dips his beak to break a strike
And Heaven spirals from a butcher's tousled tyke.

The statuary stirs. Unarmed,
The soul of piety lies down embalmed,
And men in top-hats grunt. Their assets are well farmed.

XI

Latin breeds everywhere. Incised
In gold, those Roman numerals look prized.
They're clear. But quoteful threnodies are ill-advised.

When a whole century complains
The testaments of virtue blur with stains.
An open scroll decants. Time stoops and entertains,

Versing Lucretius on a ball.
Overhead robins flaunt rust while they call.
Inversions truckle under. Pillars lean and fall.

Even the general Christian names,
Immortal from the chisel, falter. Fame's
Left for the few whose Aeneid dug deep. Lightness lames.

XII

Here an old woman bends. I nod
In passing to her, as if I were God
And she the Virgin Mary. Time mounds to a clod

Under her fingers. She looks ill
With pouring water that will always spill
Into a broken vase. She has her age to kill.

Nothing will help. Not even my hand
If I could float it on her shoulder, bland
With unforgiving interference, baked and canned.

But I'm no priest. Nor she alive
To what impinges on her tough, domed hive.
Working has stooped her old back. Elsewhere, the drones thrive.

XIII

So said my mother. But she died
 Before I realised what agony fried
The straight grain of her hair. And how her marriage lied.

It sent her someone for a life
 Whose brilliance cut her like a carving-knife.
Death, who can sharpen blades, allowed no wedded wife.

We vased lank flowers. Through the holes
 I thrust their breathing stalks, their draughty souls.
A wartime winter bit us. We fought back from Cole's

With tea and pikelets. And he flew
 To star-grit whom that grim shell chopped askew.
In the uniform of ground, so many dressed so few.

XIV

Later, she followed. And was tried
By a tribunal of the damned inside.
Her liver dried. And all one night my pity cried

Uselessly to hear her moan
Like a cow lowing as life turned to bone.
She left me nineteen years of age, and tears that groan.

I have them still. That twisting scarf
The old woman flickers as she turns to laugh
Reminds me how my heart was broken, and how half

Remains to mend. The simple ends
Of living are to make some right amends
It often seems. And a frustrated pity rends.

XV

Not always, though. Honour ascends
The rostra, and the titillating trends
Of a bitter cynicism roister. We make friends

With worms and activists. The urns
Of pity fill up with a sperm that churns.
A grey fog oozes on the Egyptian rocks and ferns.

Victoria falters. Fallen away
To leaf-mould and the loose December sway
Of weak winds, things all whisper what they used to say

Out loud. You have to float ahead
However hard it feels, leaving your dead.
On their graves, the clean feast of survival has been spread.

XVI

Reflections break. I feel a rain
Squeezed from the rafters of my tired brain
Grind on the gravel, and become real. Dogs' necks crane

Up to the sponge. Umbrellas arc
And two old men walk moulded through the dark.
A young man huddled by a shelter strikes a spark.

He smokes. They walk on, out of time,
Under their helmets of a grey, slate slime.
Puddles are dancing with rain's tilted pararhyme,

Left hand of tears. Sinister-wet,
I turn my collar up, in a cold sweat.
Fear does a rugger tackle. Stroke me like a pet.

XVII

All right. I hate the whole void place.
Its empty nullity. Its smell of grace.
Its churchy melodrama like a carapace.

Under it, things hurt. People smile
At what is (yes) unutterably vile
And a world of weeping pivots on a brace of style.

The tombs deliver. Bones are locked
Into their charnel odour. God is mocked.
The precious ointments of smarm dignity are stocked.

So pause. Let fear have its full go
Before you carve the final furbelow
And send Grace in her crinoline, to primp at Stowe.

XVIII

Vomit, or scream. Macabre stuff
It may seem to be crying, hold, enough,
Macduff-wise, and then ending in an awesome huff.

The extruded elements of fear
Or hate, the modica, dissolve, or fleer.
You do a wobbler, then you drop down frothing. Near

The hospital, the boneyard stands,
A deck of horror for a fan of hands.
Believe me. You can clog your heart with ampersands

But nothing passes. Not the tortuous buck,
At any rate, for which you need flawed luck
When all your life assembles to be graveyard-struck.

XIX

Reaching the gate, I feel rain pause.
As if subjected to their own rude laws
That mask no fragile hope. I clasp my fists like claws.

Eagles die, too. But some remain
Like figureheads that front a moving train.
Everything dies. But flowers always bloom again.

Not the same flowers. No, but flowers.
Clones of those flowers that died at other hours.
Clones, one supposes then, mask superhuman powers.

But, to be clones. To be like drones
Indistinguishable as grey stones.
Better to die, perhaps. Better to be just bones.

XX

The marching files glide slow. In state
Horror with lowered flags goes by, grown great.
The silver coins of eulogy clank on the plate.

Funerals echo. Trumpets flare
And the parade of leaving makes men stare.
To the drum-beat of tears blood monitors despair.

The heart lifts up. Widows learn how
To straighten weasel backs, small boys to bow
Fatherless heads. Prayers furrow each bereaved one's brow.

Tears know best. Stalwart in a stole
The priest prepares each coffin for its role
And ceremonies beautify a glaring hole.

XXI

Clay shears off. Somehow ritual grace
Enacts a transitory healing-space.
The broken heart is hung with jet-black mourning lace.

Shortly, the chisels chip. Grass moves
And stones absorb dull grieving to their grooves.
The Apocalyptic horses champ and stamp their hooves.

A foghorn sounds. An aeroplane
Lifts off as if to dry the Spanish main
To a cargo of spent tears, a hold of impoverished rain.

No one has energy to shriek
Even as long as half an hour a week
And frightful memories gouge trouble. Corpses reek.

THE SLAUGHTER GROUND

'An Englishman's home is not so much his castle as his chopping-block.'

– Harriette Wilson, *Memoirs*, 1825

I

When did love waver? Was it there
In Cromer, or caught helpless by the stair
Where asthma pinned you gasping? Asking sounds unfair.

The loser cringed. The winner smiled,
Bruising the flagon with her lips, too mild
To crave a proper breather. There were storm-clouds piled

Even then in the scarlet west,
The honour-field where duty lay undressed
And nothing save the need for staying close was stressed.

Things worsened, though. A baby's hand
Stood over Yarmouth, and fool's gold was fanned
Into its palms. The clockwork broke to winnowing sand.

II

Somehow the cleaver struck. The kill
Was hovering like a kestrel by the grill.
You didn't want to cook. Puddings were overspill,

Soups were a menace. Try yourself
The boredom of just standing by a shelf
Salting a pan. Try being magic, like an elf

Whenever someone wants it. Fry
Fat sausages, and learn to live and lie
Legs open with a pain that makes you want to cry.

Secrets, these: open secrets found
Under the fortress of the moles' main mound
Near to the tortured mattress of the slaughter ground,

III

Hard by the pyramid of skulls
Where Christmas wines were sluicing bowls of mulls
Too rancid to be swallowed, where a blind grape dulls

And bed seems easy, a relief
After the tension. But the pulse is brief
And nothing lasts, even this closeness known in chief,

The rock of lust. A madness comes
Out of the night of blood, like mingling rums
Inflaming anger, and a sound of hornets hums,

The buzz of quarrel. Sick, Oh, sick
Out of all bearing, so it seems, to kick
Over all trace. Where now's your boxing clever trick?

IV

Each has one. It may be just a yard
Where galvanising bins are tipped and scarred
By the claws of marauding foxes, or cats after lard.

East London shows you. Four feet square
Patches of scorched earth, Russianly bare.
Nothing grows there except the means to trap and scare.

Ants crawl at huge risk. Winter fleas
Take refuge under carpets, bite your knees.
Mounds like the hills Scott's wizard threw up rise in threes.

Hands itch. Outdoors, the killing starts.
The scattered poisons grapple for their hearts.
Our fellow creatures dodge. But the filed arrow darts.

V

Here is your killing ground: your field
Where tortoise families form a nuclear shield.
To go for the jugular's allowed. Pity's repealed.

All winter, in the shifting wind
The hunter with his shot-gun tracks the skinned,
The pitiless. Forefathers taught us that we sinned,

Now it's just crime. A poaching right
Admits the rifle's telescopic sight.
Men in dour Wellingtons wade streams. A planning blight

Affects the waving trees. Bored guns
Blazon a magnitude that folds and stuns.
Our only duty is to spare the breeding ones.

VI

We rise at breakfast, carnivore,
Tearing at bacon till our mouths grow sore
And calling for more kidney dishes, more, more, more.

Lights, guts and innards, heart
Shovelled aside, then minced up in a tart
And offal ground with bones and muffled by a fart

Thicken the brew. The inward soup
We swallow, while it swallows, in one swoop
Stops cavities of pity. Maggots loop the loop

For gristle. Beef, then dripping steaks
Anoint the dead saliva each mouth makes.
The gravy of our blood congeals in Stygian lakes.

VII

Fantasy. Well, meat-eaters break
  Wind like a gas of expectation; flake
Air with their grinders. Oh, burn Virgil at the stake

  And let the classics, cannibal
  To Dante, re-endow decide as shall.
The little people opt for Popeye as their Pal.

  It's much the same. Your side of roast
  Raw as the chicken bits they fry on toast
Appears to matter more. Each meal offloads its ghost

  Where fish-bones filter into brains
  And vegetables clog the drains
And leave a dry precipitate, like bloody stains.

VIII

All summer long, some of them rest,
Nose down in hammocks, as they appraise the Test.
The real test comes later. In a soaking vest

Up to your waist in mud, you hide
And bang away at mallard, thick with pride.
The great wings clap and falter. Nothing will abide.

Not even owls. Not even crows
That shy their battledores in blackened rows
Across the fragile oaks. Tickets are sold for those.

The train of your destruction trails.
Wide modern farming has you on the rails.
Knights in grey armour fossilise. None own to Grails.

IX

Here in the pleasaunce of the fens
A startling expedition shoos the hens.
Rising at six, men plunge out. Ermine, botched in dens,

Go to the ground. The proper ground
For killing these is feeding the flapped hound
That scours them up. But now for fun some fop's fur-crowned.

The badger settle, disappear.
Nothing but heron risk a living near;
Nothing but pheasant that can roost in trees. Oh, hear

You pheasants, though. The glorious day
Is coming when the guns will slice your play,
The permissive twelfth. The day when shire knights rise to slay.

X

Anger gropes under. And the fish
Dips in the current for a tasty dish.
They flit as minnows, delicates. While all they wish,

Those fishermen, the rods of souls,
Is that no day will ever bring controls.
The Christian spirit flickers. Dear Christ, those gouged holes!

Kingfishers dive. But human hooks
Rake like a callous on the skin of brooks.
Flies rise. The dragonflies above them stoop like cooks

Watching a meal heat. Azure flash
Indicates gauze on water, sausage hash.
The gutted trout that swam the Torridge lies like trash.

XI

Death's easy. Why, to slay a slug
All that you need is bootsoles, and a rug.
The operation takes five seconds, and a shrug.

They trail in on your shoe; crawl down
And wave their horns. You orchestrate a frown.
The cats all stare in disbelief. The leaf is brown

He races for. Too late. The fold
Of intervening softness is uprolled.
The rubber poises. And the lethal googly's bowled.

Messy, you say. Well, some like mess.
The honourable muck of their distress
Reprieves a too-clean conscience, bleeding to undress.

XII

The little folk shove in. Their homes
Exfoliate with crocketing and domes.
We can kill, too. Our mousetraps click like metronomes.

We'll drown the spiders, and you brain
The woolly mammoth, and the whooping-crane.
Divide the work. Allow us beetles, and a drain.

You can have sand-pits, lorry-loads
Of beaters, and a choice of Borneo roads.
We'll take the swatter, and annihilate the toads.

It's easy. Kill and cure, we say.
Particulars evade. The general sway
Drops for extermination. Moles' skulls deck a tray.

XIII

So, countrified and sad, I blame
The citadel of truth, the slaying-game.
The television aerial plays it cool. The same

Carnage is dire in Israel.
In Lebanon they sound the slavering-bell
That leashes teeth for meat. Oh, crucify it well.

Unjust. It is, indeed, unjust
When every sentinel whom we can trust
Alerts us from a column. Pigeons who pout their bust

Coo for deliverance. The can
Has to be carried. Shit will hit the fan.
And the betrayed and threatened species now is, Man.

XIV

The cruising dart-men in the sky
Mouth at the sliding gun-ports while we die.
Pushing through undergrowth I sense their shadow fly.

I pause. Look up, and see your God
White as good linen, or a side of cod.
He fires. You tumble down; and dream you kiss the rod.

At school, we'd knock at bats with bats.
I'd swipe at them with well-oiled willow. Hats
Off for a score. I was Don Bradman, but in spats.

That was a sport; a Harrow thing
When summer evenings bent a broken wing.
The turrets darkened. Then the battleaxe would swing.

XV

Thus many. But the mood has changed.
A certain amnesty has been arranged.
Promiscuous culling's over. All that was deranged.

Of course, we've got to care. Tongues wag
Like pendula. It leaves a decent bag.
Heads choke the wall. Moth-eaten bearskins leer and brag.

Here in my own hall, shield-backed skulls
I didn't shoot manoeuvre like braced hulls..
What was their pulling-power once is what still hauls and
                                                    culls.

I keep them for a show. Ashamed
Is what I ought to be to see them tamed.
Outdoors, the roebuck leap. Here ancestors are framed.

XVI

Night has a hold, though. In its mist
I walk some distance from the quarry I missed.
Sweet, poising house. Your twin towers perch along my wrist

Like falcons, and I feel their claws.
In the dark wood a mating barn-owl saws.
Nothing is left to alter but the assumed applause.

A gargoyle stops me, lolls its tongue
Like a lion's, modestly but heavily hung.
I drink its flashback like a great bell's clapper swung.

This is the past. Religions grin
Against their mediaeval origin
Where lust and anarchy broke wind, then belched a gin.

XVII

Empire was all. King Edward spoke
  And eighty lions roared. On hearts of oak
Our cold ships broke the seas, and steam was raised with coke.

  Another kind of coke remains.
  It satisfies what energy explains,
The easy transference of empire. First, the plains

  Take out the bison, then their braves,
  The flag advances over bursting graves.
The Union Jack's starred back bears stripes now, like a slave's.

  Well. It was over with the war.
  After the bulls and bears had stocked the floor
The footmen left. America was shown the door.

XVIII

But was she? She came back for more
Touting an ancestry that knew the gore.
In cowboy accents, gangsters practised to adore.

Halls fall. The great estates all kneel
And shooting-lodge by shooting-lodge they squeal.
The absentees, on heat for money, do a deal.

Scotland fares worst. The failing grouse
Require more capital to forge their house.
Dollars restore old stag-hunts. Proud as a stuffed mouse

The new earl settles. Greenbacks move
From bank to bank like finches. Banks approve.
Money should move. The blood of shot birds oils the groove.

XIX

Here by the Ouse, I buck the trend,
Or wish I could, near to a new year's end.
Nothing seems possible, save spend and spend and spend.

Exhausted by inaction, numb,
The passengers for isolation come.
I hear their plane's roar, like a helicopter's hum.

Shall I be one? Retreat, or die.
Learn to be easy with the wind-swept sky
And watch the clouds build higher, while trees toss and shy.

The long year darkens. And the time
For drawing down the curtains brings thick rime.
The glacial windows creak, marred with an icy grime.

XX

Pale domesticity fares worst.
In winter my poor Troubles slakes his thirst
Under brave chicken-wire. His bob-tailed life seems cursed.

Wait for the Bomb. If shadowing fire
Sundered the Custom's House at King's Lynn, ire
Would roll like lava to embroil us all in mire.

Things in their cages, things we hold
We sacrifice for freedom from the cold.
They would be first to die. So gather force, be bold.

Stiff peacocks and tame rabbits, yield.
Rough spaniels and wry cats, patrol the field.
Fate has a strange, dark passport signed and safely sealed.

XXI

Enter its aura. Here the womb
Opens to show its coffered honeycomb.
Sweetness is broached with light, like Tutankhamen's tomb.

A dark child rises. Grey as bees
The blood of ages boils about his knees
Where teak-woods more archaic than Guyana's freeze.

I touch his bones. Grandfathers die.
One's blood moon-rockets to the Shotts-bred sky.
The other's gathers like a drip-feed, hung to dry.

Birth is a long-clear building-site
Where half the labour force in love with white
Builds for the other half, their faces black with light.

XXII

Will they do better? Who can guess
Watching the march of Libya, and the mess.
Abroad, the scimitar anneals. At home, distress.

Here in the ghettoes, numbness drains
In an oblivion of men with brains
Who have to crawl for money. No one thinks or strains.

Flat noses rule. Crisp hair's in vogue.
The pale executives are reading Logue
But every other rastafarian's a rouge,

Some say. No job is going soon
For anyone whose mum's an octaroon.
The dole's doled out like gruel, from a sterling spoon.

XXIII

Is Christianity a grain
Where darkness hooks for moth-balls like a crane?
Gold was a blossom once. Now it seems just a pain.

Here the proud empire like a purse
Empties its hoard of copper for a curse
And London seethes with prejudice. Wiggenhall's worse.

Even the body of a child
Whose flaxen hair shone whiter than the wild
Lily, the Christmas rose, would feel the cold slurs piled.

Mine has. I write his proper name
Here for an honour to the Grecian flame.
I see him crucified and being black his blame.

XXIV

Rhetoric shades. If this were true
Then Alexander's would be Christ's cross, too,
And sparse Greek riddles sieve the bible through and through.

They don't. Black faces tour the streets
And babies like their fathers gorge on meats.
Brixton is far from Wiggenhall. But the same stew heats

The firebrands. And the same rage burns.
The same solstitial remedy interns
And the same need for comfort every night returns.

Eat meat, and live. Kill, and be killed.
The cemeteries like hospitals are filled.
Each slaughterground's a school. Smithfield's the place we
                                                    willed.

XXV

Look in the fire. Brown wood-lice burn
Who lived in peace like suckers under fern;
Whose final torchlight sutra now no eyes discern.

Why do I say, who? Why not, which?
The reasons belly in the flames, too rich
To be believed. Do central nervous systems twitch?

Oh, no. Just, movement makes me cry,
Knowing the heat, guessing the fumes, and why
They have to be exposed to searing pain and die.

Why, to make me warm: so that I
Can live in peace, poor sucker, while I fry;
So that a human being may be calm and dry.

XXVI

This afternoon I cut my thumb
And dressed it like a rose. Now it feels numb
And shines red through the plaster like a rugger scrum.

Bad periods glow thus. A rose
Bears dark reminders that it may dispose.
Where is the great, good place? Where do live adders doze

In uncreated warmth, and calm
Extend all round their coiling like an arm
And nothing, wing nor beak, approach them to bring harm?

I ask the rose to open, drive
Grief back, and leave the burning lice alive.
I want the price of murder to be thews that thrive.

XXVII

Outdoors, a majesty of rings
Adorns the fretwork lace that winter strings.
But frost is severed by the clock, like unbound springs.

The water moves. The broad ice cracks.
The moon's arc is a driven battleaxe
That cuts the stars to fragments in the tractor's tracks

Furrowing soil for winter wheat
While farming shreds the sunlight for its heat
And something turns in pain and staggers to its feet

And shrugs, and grows to meat. This year
Blood is the heritage all have to fear.
But blood is eaten, blood is drunk. Blood fats the steer.

XXVIII

The garden is the great divide
The cleaver settles to, and shares with pride.
The slaughter-pool brings whirring wings. Blood packs the hide.

Blood is my creed. I cry for blood
As female robins twitter for a stud.
I watch my rose turn sanguinary from blood's bud.

Outdoors on snow the red mists rise.
The crimson of charisma blinds my eyes
To what is rancid offal, and is choked with flies.

I sniff the wind, use my new nose
And douse its tube of polyps with a dose
Of gamey air. This world of blood stinks like a rose.